W9-BBQ-212

Eight Monologues
from *Americana West*

Red Shuttleworth

Sept. 19, 2019

To Lynn,
Best Wishes,
Red

Humanitas Media Publishing

Copyright © Red Shuttleworth. All Rights Reserved.

CAUTION:

All inquiries for the use of any part of this book, any of the monologues in *Eight Monologues from Americana West,* in any manner whatsoever, should be addressed to the author, Red Shuttleworth: redshuttleworth@gmail.com; or to Kirk Ellis: kellis1848@aol.com.

ACKNOWLEDGMENTS:

The *Americana West: A Century of Short Plays and Monologues* project could not have been written without a 2017 Tanne Foundation Award.

I deeply appreciate the collaboration with Kirk Ellis. His advice and work were invaluable.

The front cover photo, back cover cast photo and all the interior photographs are by Ciara Shuttleworth… except the interior author photograph, which is by Steve Rimple.

Back cover photo: The original cast for *Eight Monologues from Americana West* and the playwright and the director: Carol Markstrom, Mark C. Jackson, Kellen Cutsforth, Micki Fuhrman, Robert Nott, Sheila Ellis, Johnny D. Boggs, Chris Enss, Red Shuttleworth, and Kirk Ellis.

For

Ciara

Kirk and Sheila

Anita and Tim

The WWA Players, on behalf of Western Writers of America, presented the world premiere of *Eight Monologues from Americana West* in the Grand Palace Saloon Theater in Old Tucson on June 21, 2019. The monologues were directed by Kirk Ellis.

The original cast was as follows:

Sonny	Robert Nott
Pablo	Mark C. Jackson
Adella	Chris Enss
Electa	Carol Markstrom
Lester	Kellen Cutsforth
Florence	Micki Fuhrman
Dana	Johnny D. Boggs
Ursula	Sheila Ellis

Director's Note

"The West" is not fixed in a single era or place. It is as much a landscape of the mind as one of physical geography, constantly evolving as perceptions of history and identity shape and re-shape our understanding. The characters in these eight short plays are American dreamers who find their respective Western myths tested, challenged and sometimes broken by Western reality. Like all great playwrights, Red Shuttleworth turns genre inside-out and gives it vital new meaning.

Kirk Ellis

A coyote pup cries and whines
near our bedroom window.
An orphan.

Contents

Cereal box toy cowboy,
canal-drowned rattlers,
drunken morticians at the Elks:
every decision feels sure and permanent.
Oh, to be a drifter in Old Tucson.

1919: Tinnie, New Mexico

(*Ranch house parlor: common desk, coiled decorative rope on a wall, a running iron also mounted on a wall. Sonny, age 39, enters and spins a wooden desk chair, looks at the audience. Sonny takes off an old campaign hat, sets it on a hat/coat tree. He is in an off-white long-sleeved shirt, dark tie, dark blue denim trousers, and boots.*)

Name's Sonny. My momma named me Sonny Kid. Sonny Kid McCarty.

Momma was part Mescalero… died of influenza last year. Lot of people killed by that flu. It's gone now, but it's gonna come back. That flu knows this country well, so it's gonna kill more souls.

Death is common in this here Lincoln County. Always been that way. I'm a businessman, so I make plans. The world requires plans.

The man I am told was my daddy... he was born in a New York City Irish slum. His proper name was Henry. Henry McCarty.

I was born in 1880.

Daddy and Momma met at a wedding dance over in Fort Sumner, but they never married. Daddy loved to dance, make love to the ladies, but he didn't take a wife.

So far... I ain't taken a wife neither.

Daddy was dead at age 21... in 1880. That makes me 39. Maybe I'll get me a homely mail order bride from New

York. Maybe I'll keep from marriage another horse's lifetime.

I'm a cattleman. Got me this small hill country ranch. Yes, sir, Daddy never owned nothin'. But I got a few acres.

Got me a Winchester, too, 'n a couple of six-shooters. Now... I do not go showin' off my six-shooters. That gets a man trouble. Never cause jealousy neither. For instance, I could have better, stronger working pens for cattle... could build a better horse corral.

I am what you might think of as a cattle business middle man. I avoid trouble when I can. Daddy... he liked trouble, 'cause it was a mirthful thing... fine for laughs. Daddy found so much trouble that.... Okay... to tell the truth... I am a

<u>rustler</u>. I take other men's cattle…
outside Lincoln County. I take cattle
and I rebrand 'em.

(*Sonny takes the running iron from the
wall.*)

This here iron… it's a runnin' iron…
and I have artistic skills. I can change
any brand to my brand. So, I guess, in
my own way, I'm trouble.

Daddy got into so much trouble that he
changed his name from Henry McCarty
to… William H. Bonney… better known
in them days as… <u>Billy the Kid</u>. (*Pause.*)
Don't believe me? I hardly believe it
myself. But Momma, she said…. And I
do favor him.

So I've built a small ranch with rustlin'
money. You need 6,000 acres in this

country to run just a hundred head. But in the cow rustlin' trade, it's about turnover.

Last year I went to St. Louis… to see the factory where they make the Dorris Delivery Van. I was tempted to buy one. You drive cattle with horses, cattle lose weight. Someday real soon… they's gonna be cattle trucks. That's where it's headed.

Raidin'… rustlin' are trades with dignity… because, unlike banking or school teaching, my line of work takes gumption and daring.

I'm 39. Maybe at 60 I'll take a wife… to keep me young 'n daring… and it might be another man's wife that I'll rustle away.

1929: Cherry, Arizona

(Front porch of a mountain shack…
corroding metal roof. Pablo, 55, is sitting
on a rickety bench, eating beans and biscuits
from a tin dish, drinking from a tin cup. He
is in old, torn denim jeans and shirt, boots,
and a frayed, bent cowboy hat.)

Times pass. People pass. The land
abides… unless there are so many mines
in its hills that it all falls into itself at
first shrug. That is what an earthquake
is… God having himself a shrug.

Times pass. Wyatt Earp passed… died
back in January. Course, Earp's Arizona
days were way south of here. But this
here town of Cherry…. Well, Cherry
was a booming mine town when Earp
and the Earp brothers and Doc Holliday
were carousing Tombstone.

Cherry, Arizona, ain't Tombstone. The
few of us here, we tell each other that

this locale is like any ol' other place. Maybe. Maybe not.

I was born in 1874, when Wyatt Earp was a young man... when he was fit and quick and strong with a fine prostate gland... with a power-stream of piss.

My daddy was in Uvalde in 1873... a cowboy. He was a one-thumb Irishman. That's what my mother told me. Sullivan was the name... and that's supposedly Irish. Anyway... like a lot of people, ol' Sullivan disappeared.

My first gal scavenged junk yards in San Antonio. We lived in a shack made from old buckets, dirt-filled burlap sacks, wrecked automobiles... that kind of stuff. She called herself Elena. Horse threw her... stepped on her ribs. Elena.

The next pair of gals were not memorable. Though I did marry one of them. Married does not make memory certain.

Life alone is bearable. Habits or no habits. Habits, tequila or smokes, habits get to be expensive.

Want to quit your tobacco? Easy 'nuff. Just promise yourself you'll only smoke cigs taken from a rich man's parlor. Not a rich man's parlor here in Cherry. Anyway, the point is to make each cigarette carry an immediate price.

My mother said to me when I turned fifteen, "Pablo," she said, "know all the ingredients on a dish, Pablo."

What? What ingredients? What dish?

I'm 55. I may never leave Cherry. Oh, I might slide down to Lonesome Valley for supplies… for a Fourth of July, for a gander at the last true old pioneers, dumb-sitting in rockers at the Pioneers Home.

I might stay here and just stink inside until I die, just stink until Jesus returns. Rot 'n stink 'n "Hello ol' Jesus… and where's the Kingdom?"

If the ingredients were ever on my plate, I never once't seen 'em, much less tasted any fancy hotel restaurant stew.

That was the Earp brothers' problem. They thought they was better… thought they could skip the beans and go straight to thick, fatty-tender cow steak.

But biscuits 'n beans…. Biscuits 'n beans can keep a man afoot for a hundred years… keep a man ready to discover a river or a vein of gold.

1961: Beach, North Dakota

(*Funeral home visitation parlor: a simple wood coffin is set on a pair of trestle sawhorses. The coffin is open. Adella, 30's, is sitting beside the coffin in an upholstered chair. She has tissue paper and is making paper carnations and placing them in a wicker basket. Adella is in a navy blue lace flare A-line dress with matching shoes. She sets aside her work.*)

I can never make up my mind. Reno or Hollywood… sometimes I consider New York.

What's in it for me at home, here in Golden Valley County, North Dakota?

I have gained my thirties. Too late in life?

Well…. It's sure too damned late for Mr. Thaddeus in his simple wood casket. Cancer of the throat. Mr.

Thaddeus was my teacher back in high school, social studies. He'd go outside, even in a blizzard, to smoke a cig 'tween classes. Then he quit smokin', became a chain chewer of hard breath-candies. Later he took to chewing unlit cigars. Never married. Has a sister in Glendive. What-all gave him cancer?

Back to me. If I was to go, where should I go? New York? It's all the "New Frontier," ain't it? Kennedy and Johnson. Kennedy is cute. But I voted Nixon... in my intentions I voted for Nixon.

Confession: I did not bother voting.

Voting…. Voting gets serious… competitive. Just ask me about that. I ran for Golden Valley Rodeo Queen. Back a few years. Rodeo Queen Princess was all I got… even after I skinnied into tight vanilla-white jeans, blood-crimson boots, and a cherry-yoke

satin cowgirl shirt I wore unsnapped
enough so men could see my
Maidenform. Some rancher's girl, a
butterball, small boobs and big belly....
That fatty got to be queen. That's voting
for you: rigged. I got runner-up... and
runner-up ain't nothin'.

And who wants runner-up when the
prize is an opportunity to marry a
wheat farmer?

Teddy Roosevelt's old ranch ain't far.
So this is the real West, not TV West.
You'd think we'd have men who can
generate some desperado daredevilry.

I want something... something
cinnamon before I age into my autumn.

Look at Mr. Thaddeus in his plain ol'
wood casket. At the end, what does he
get? He gets me, funeral parlor
receptionist... working her way up to
funeral parlor consultant. He gets me,

Adella, his former student. Mr.
Thaddeus gets me for last company, me
making red 'n white paper carnations to
fill up all the remaining space in the
casket.

Nothing stays on the sly, right? All
secrets get gossiped-out. They divorce
horses, don't they? But... Mr.
Thaddeus... poor fellow... no rumors.
He was an upright man all his solitary
life. No fun.

No mistakes. All fun begins with
mistakes. And mistakes begin with
someone sayin', "I love you."

If someone can't make a mistake with
me, if some man can't sweetly say, "I
love you," then it might be time for me
to leave the Badlands.

Or maybe it's time for me to stop being
picky... time for me to say, "I love you,"

to a lonesome rancher in these lonesome parts.

Look at Mr. Thaddeus. Alone with high school teaching. Sucking cigs, sucking hard candies, chewin' unlit cigars.

Shoot, Mr. Thaddeus, let me say this to you, if only for my own practice, "I love you."

(Adella pours her wicker basket of paper carnations into the coffin.)

1971: Liberal, Kansas

(*Dust-brown plowed ground… endless, flat horizon. Electa, 40, is plodding along, costumed in a 1971 white Allen B. Shepard NASA Astronaut walk-on-the-moon white suit, sans helmet. She stops.*)

Here we are. Northwest of town. Just off a ways from Bird Road… in some farmer's ripped, powdery, dust-dry ground.

Soil matters. Dust is vital. If there's nothing to hold it down, soil blows away. That is a harsh lesson… the Dust Bowl lesson. These farmers were taught it. But, except for shelter trees around farmhouses, you'd be hard-pressed to locate a tree near Liberal, Kansas.

The wind blows… dirt moves. Wind blows… people move. Like I moved here two years ago… when they started the junior college… Seward County

Community College. Forest green and white. The Saints. The Saints? Saints like the local farmers were Catholics or Mormons. I suppose there's a difference, but I don't give a hoot. Because I'm a scientist. Well… not exactly a scientist… only a woman with a master's degree in biology from a mid-level state college.

So I was hired to teach junior college transfer level science.

This astronaut outfit: I had the college buy it. Mail order space exploration is huge. And it's easier to get a properly fitted astronaut suit than it is to get a well-fitting bra. That's another story.

So… when my husband ran off to be a San Francisco poet… more recently a failed poet making watercolor paintings on the Mendocino coast… with all that, I needed a job.

Never imagined I'd turn forty traipsing through the abused soil of some Kansas farmer. This was old Comanche ground... Suitable for bison. Not naturally suited for farming.

All the water comes from wells. Wells sunk into the Ogallala Aquifer. Mark my word: the wells will go dry in less than a century.

And when the wells around here blow air and blow grit instead of water, no number of Hail Marys will make much difference. The wind will blow.

Just as the wind is blowing right now... lightly out of the northwest. And you can sure catch a nasty whiff of Denver... air pollution. And Denver is 350 miles away by buzzard flight.

Here we are... just outside Liberal. And they situated the junior college between a country club and a landfill. Imagine that as a message.

And imagine me, a forty-year-old science schoolmarm, divorced in Kansas. Maybe like an astronaut walking the moon and meeting her next husband.

It's best, particularly in a second marriage, to find a man with <u>lineage</u>… with pride of history… with something to live up to.

My father wasn't much of a baseball player. He was what you might call a half-talent. But my father got to play some minor league professional baseball. He was lucky one year to be in spring training with the New York Yankees.

My father is seventy-one. To this day, when he meets someone new, my father says, "Shake the hand that shook the

hand of Babe Ruth." That is <u>lineage</u>.
How many can say they associated with
a great person, with a person of
achievement?

So the last creature I'd marry, first or
later marriage, would be a junior college
president. Because JUCO presidents
stink of bad electrical wiring... glad-
handers... closet booze-hounds. And
they have no lineage. Not even the half-
talent of semi-achievers. No. I will not
take romantic dinner with a junior
college president, nor a vice president,
nor a dean.

My parents named me <u>Electa</u>... for some
mystical not-quite-named woman... a
mother in the Bible. What a stretch, eh?

Electa. My mom and dad used to say,
"You can <u>Electa</u> your fate." That is true
and not true, though we certainly get
many of the fruits of our elections.

Yet... there is also Brownian Movement,
random movement of heated molecules.

Maybe this is all random... me taking
the weekend afternoon air... strolling on
a moon called Kansas... in an astronaut
suit bought with junior college money to
entertain bored eighteen year olds.
Discovery on the High Plains!

(*She picks up a handful of powdery soil, lets
it slip between her fingers.*)

1974: Plainview, Texas

(A treeless plain. In the distance, a dead-stopped center pivot, reddish-brown dirt, a few sparse weeds. Lester, 20's, enters, dressed in jeans, denim shirt, boots, old straw cowboy hat.)

I'm waiting for the well-drillin' rig. Be along soon.

Here... just out of Plainview, water has to be drilled for. Only rains a half-dozen inches a year.

This here's the Llano Estacado. The Staked Plains. Great American Desert. Olden days Comanche country... but them Comanche knew better than to live here. Yep. The Comanche only used the Llano Estacado to pass through.

So today we'll start a new job... drillin' water for some farmer who's gonna reap as much water as he can... for

cotton, or wheat, or corn… or pretty
sunflowers.

Yep. We're gonna drill him some water.

The water is from something called the
Ogallala Aquifer. Up north, up
Nebraska way, I hear it's an
underground lake.

Down here in northwest Texas, the
Ogallala Aquifer is a series of streams…
maybe one time underground rivers.
Now they're smaller streams. Imagine
more wells… thousands more wells
sucking water from these streams.

Early explorers saw that these plains
were uninhabited. And they reckoned
this country would all stay uninhabited.

No water… no habitation.

But nowadays we got drills and wells
and big pipes.

Now we got Lubbock. We got Amarillo.
We got your Midland and Odessa. And
barely out of sight of where I'm
standing, we got your Plainview.

In only a hundred years, about year
2074, the water is gonna be gone. These
wells that I help drill… they's gonna
blow air 'n grit.

So who you gonna blame when the
Llano Estacado goes back to being a
barren plain of bleached bone and piles
of dried cow scours and petrified
buffalo shit… when this ground is
moon-like?

Blame. Sometimes we can't… can't
point fingers at who wronged us.

Long ago there was this boy….

And this boy reached his eleventh
birthday… just as his momma and
newest step-daddy and his eight sisters

and brothers were movin'... drivin' an ol' station wagon from San Angelo north to... north to... north. See, that boy turned eleven and his momma and the new step-daddy did <u>not</u> tell him where-all they was movin' to.

So... this station wagon, filled with an American family, pulls into Plainview, Texas, parks near the Fair Theater... near that soda parlor that used to be on or near Broadway.

And to the boy's surprise, he gets told to climb out of the station wagon. His momma gets out of the car, too. They walk to the soda parlor... and....

Okay, look, this is my story. I won't fool you.

My momma takes me to the soda parlor... buys me an ice cream cone... vanilla with chocolate sauce.

Momma explains: the family's broke.
They'll stand a better chance… if I stay
behind. Momma's cryin'. Sobbin'. And
she walks us south on Broadway…
walks us to the old Hilton Hotel.

Ten or so years back, the Hilton was a
big time hotel… a place for oilmen to
party for days.

My momma says to me, "Lester, a lot of
Christians come to Plainview. One a
them will adopt you. You tell what we
had to do… leave you behind… 'cause
we're so desperate.

My new step-daddy had the station
wagon parked across from the Hilton.
Momma walked to the car. She looked
back as the car rolled away. Only a
mother looks back. I waved.

I walked into the Hilton… into the
lobby. None of the guests took a shine

to me. Before long, a bellhop kicked my
ass to the gutter.

So maybe now you'll understand: when
the cities of the Llano Estacado run out
of well water, folks will drive away... a
few with money and where-with-all.
Some sorry people will drive off... leave
behind kin that they claim to love.

Such is human nature.

Me... I'm gonna help drill a water well
where there soon won't be water.

End of the month comes, I'll buy T-
bones, cartons of frozen veggies...
couple cases of longnecks... a bottle of
tequila. I won't look back. Most of us
don't look back... not very far.

And when all the water is pumped out
of the last underground streamlets of
the Ogallala Aquifer, maybe only forty
years from now, I won't feel at all guilty.

I'll just take my saved-up wages… climb into my pickup… and I'll drive… like some drunk ol' honky tonk man… gettin' what might pass for a last laugh.

1976: Rattlesnake Station, Idaho

(A gravel wayside with a commemorative marker on Sun Valley Road a few miles north of Mountain Home. In the distance is a buckled 'n broken stone schoolhouse. Florence, 30's, is leaning against the front hood of an early seventies Cadillac. She's eating from a sack of fries, drinking from a quart bottle of beer. Florence is in a maxi gown with spaghetti straps, white "sweet sixteen" cowgirl boots, and a white Stetson.)

I got myself a road trip life. That's what this is. Nothin' like driving the West. It's real. It's sudden and real. Like being on-the-run. Rivers of blacktop… August sunlight.

Deserts of desire. Most folks drive right past desire.

Then there's the going home. Or deeper: there's the going home to origins.

Like this here roadside cut-out northeast of Mountain Home. Mountain Home is an Idaho crossroads... mostly supported by interstate drivers... and the Air Force base.

So Mountain Home has a honky tonk. Once a year I pass through... take a weekend gig... singing... singing in a club for airmen... singing my versions of "Rhinestone Cowboy," "You Sure Hank Done It This Way," and singing Loretta, 'n Tanya, 'n Linda Ronstadt.

It's a dollar. It's gas and burger money. It is freedom.

And I am free. Like Billy Joe sings, "Bein' free ain't too much to be."

So once a year, I cruise up this road, Sun Valley Road, or Road #20 if you insist.

Once a year I pull over, stop here. This roadside marker says this empty place

was once Rattlesnake Station… a
booming stage coach rest stop.

My grandparents, my daddy's parents,
they were born here… up that hill… up
past that buckled 'n broken stone
schoolhouse. My great grandparents…
they were pioneers. Settlers. They died
young 'n poor… owing money on
skeleton-cattle they were trying to ranch
with. My great grandparents' Ol' West
was a losing proposition. A life of
sucking on winterkill cow bones.

Imagine that instead of burgers 'n fries,
imagine suckin' 'n gnawin' some cow
that died of cold or froze… with its ass-
end eaten to a bloody crater by coyotes.

That is not my world. My world
includes sequins, rhinestones, satin
cowgirl shirts unsnapped to aquamarine
push-up bras… and drunks trying to
sing along.

My world is rough on sleep, but it sure beats the humdrum of bein' a filin' clerk with a moldy ol' Denver apartment... and it sure must beat keepin' a neat house for some Salt Lake City holier-than-thou.

The West. Better to be a photo album cowboy than to sell insurance in Boise.

Maybe I got romantic notions. Maybe 'cause my parents named me Florence... for the town in Italy. Florence. They got a postcard from Italy before I was born... so I got to be called Florence. Or Flo for short... as in go-with-the-flow.

Tell you what: only divorce can bring a girl of eighteen to truth. That was my case, so for me... divorce was a truth.

I love Willie 'n Waylon as much as y'all do. But I refuse to be a good-hearted woman in love with a two-timin' man... and I refuse to pretend interest in some

man's crappy day. I do not wash
windows, do not shop for chicken pot
pie, and I do not sew cute baby clothes
out of big ol' flour sacks. I do not want
to endlessly wrangle about whose turn
it is to cook supper or wash the dishes. I
like men fine, but I like a bed to
myself... no nocturnal farts but my own.

Sometimes, sure, I think I might want to
be a momma. There's still time. Don't
go tellin' me what I already know: the
hands of the clock tremble and we get
old. You okay with that? I sure am.

My chances of bein' a singin' star, now
that I have crossed the river into my
thirties... my chances are slim. But I am
out here... free... gettin' my kicks...
infatuated with bad, pot-hole,
washboard roads.
Maybe someday I'll have me an Idaho
front porch swing, south of the lights of
Boise, off that two-lane to Elko.

Maybe someday I'll have enough money laid back… and maybe I'll have blueberries 'n whipped cream mornings. Maybe.

Maybe I'll be killed in a head-on four in the morning crash.

It's all luck, ain't it? Wish me some luck.

(*She lifts the bottle of beer to her mouth, drinks. She sets the bottle down on the hood of the car… yodels.*)

1978: Hettinger, North Dakota

(The county sheriff's office: grey metal desk, a file cabinet, wall calendar, and an end table holding a jade plant decorated with tiny Christmas lights. Dana, 50's, is at his desk, writing. An upturned hat rests on the table. He rotates once in his old wooden chair, goes back to writing. Dana is in a tan lawman's shirt with a badge, jeans, boots. Dana stops writing, pulls a six-pack of Coke cans from under his desk, pops one open. He takes a gulp, spins around, faces downstage.)

Happy Thanksgiving from Adams County, North Dakota.

I don't mind working two shifts today… to give a couple of my men some family time.

I like family time, but not at Thanksgiving. Because I hate turkey. If I was home, my wife, Cindy… she would try to convert me to turkey appreciation. Turkey. Never eat what's been washed in its own blood 'n pus, piss 'n shit.

Thanksgiving: a great night for ambulance calls... mostly heart attacks... gluttony heart attacks.

You even get close to Thanksgiving and Mr. Death comes to visit.

Two nights ago, the Laws (real names), Bob and Barbi Law throw a party at their over-mortgaged cow operation. They splurge. Lots of steaks to broil. Case or two of whiskey and Russian vodka.

Now... Bob's a huge baseball fan. Loves the Yankees... Billy Martin plus those '61 boys led by Roger Maris, who is from North Dakota. So Bob loves Roger Maris. Maris is long gone. Even Mickey Mantle is gone. But Bob loves the

Yankees and he's so glad they had Billy Martin as manager, but Billy was fired... and this year it was Bob Lemon who managed the Yankees to the Series win.

Now, Barbi... Mrs. Law, she doesn't want to hear any more about the Yankees. She's throwing a pre-Thanksgiving steak feast 'n booze blow-out... one the Laws can't afford. She's hard-pressed.

The party starts around noon. People from Hettinger... Adams County... good ranch and farm people.

(*Pause. He drinks some Coke.*)

Problems out at the Laws' ranch are not rare.

Barbi and Bob. Well... holidays are hazards. Last 4th of July they got to drinkin' after the fireworks. Barbi hits Bob behind the right ear with a beer bottle. He's bleeding when one of my deputies arrives, bleeding and holding a kitchen towel to his head. So… Bob declines prosecution. Yep… Bob does not want Barbi cuffed and dragged away. We interview Barbi later… and she has no memory of how her Bob got conked on the head.

(*Pause. He drinks more Coke… puts in a pinch of Copenhagen, spits tobacco juice into his trash can.*)

About a year ago, a deputy responds to the Law's place. Bob Law has been stabbed in the upper gut region. Bob refuses medical treatment when the meat wagon arrives. But then… I was on hand, too. Bob is full of pioneer spirit. He says to me, "It's only a bitty puncture. Bulls have done worse to me." Rumor here in Hettinger is that Bob Law threatened to slash Barbi's tires… because she is always driving off to church. Yeah… the old excuse of "church."

So… two nights back, Bob Law is lecturing one and all on the Yankees, Billy Martin… and Roger Maris.

We get a call. Barbi is sobbin'. County dispatch almost can't understand Barbi. She's weepin'. She says, "My Bob… my Bob… he's very sick… he's bleedin'."

Okay… so I reckon I'll take this call. I get out there with the ambulance right behind me. Guests have dispersed.

They're in the parlor, Bob 'n Barbi. Lot of framed magazine covers of Yankees, a shelf of autographed baseballs in plastic cubes.

Bob is in his recliner… lookin' pale… lookin' like he's lost a lot of blood. Actually… Bob looks dead. And his Barbi… well, Barbi is crying to Bob, trying to hug his torso from the sides of the La-Z-Boy recliner. She's cryin', "I'm sorry… I'm so sorry."

Bob… he's got stab wounds to the right shoulder, to his left arm, and in the left armpit. And Bob's stabbed in the rear left shoulder area.

Coroner calls me later, tells me that Bob's body is scarred… and not from his being a white boy doing the Sun Dance. Nope. It was a marital practice with Barb 'n Bob… her stabbin' and him forgiving.

Me? I avoid as much marital conflict as I can. Let someone else eat the hot turkey, let someone else empty an entire can of whipped cream on a single slice of store-bought pumpkin pie.

I'd rather work Thanksgiving… drink some Coke, dip Copenhagen snuff…

and just sit 'n spit… wait for someone to be killed.

(Dana tosses the snuff can into the upturned hat, takes a swig of Coke.)

1994: Shoshone, California

(A ramshackle trailer kitchen with pink walls, a metal/Formica-top table. Ursula, 50's, is at the table in front of a small make-up mirror. She wears an old bathrobe and a terrycloth turban.)

Nothing ages me all that much. I look real good... firm-for-fifties.

I'm a Death Valley waitress. P.O. box here in Shoshone. Got this double-wide trailer... and it's nearly paid clear. There's worse off 'n me. I get good tips. Great tips from bikers. Families don't tip good. Families are wore-out, especially second 'n third marriage families.

Off days, I take the half hour drive over to Pahrump... visit the Smith's grocery store... buy what I might itch for... throw a couple handfuls of quarters into the slots.

Grocery store slot machines won't kill you. Last three years of slots on a Wednesday…. Well, I am only fifty-seven dollars behind. Fifty-seven dollars in losses ain't all that bad. It's entertainment.

I met this man over in Pahrump last Wednesday. Fellow in his prime years… maybe with a military retirement.

This guy has got this big dog. Half Great Dane. Half Pit Bull. He can't let this dog run loose, not ever, 'cause the dog has put a bite on seven people already. Including the business license woman in Pahrump. She's a former "nice girl" at Sheri's Ranch. This man owns a fast-print shop. So, one day, this woman strolls into the print shop and proceeds to talk in a loud, demanding voice.

Now the dog, this Great Dane and goddamned Pit Bull, thinks he owns the place. So, what do you think he does? He takes a bite of that old whore's ass!

The man, he told me all this. I was at the Pahrump Community Swimming Pool. It's got six lanes. Anyway... this man with the big dog... he and I were swimming laps.

Later I see this man as he's walking his yellow, huge-headed dog. The man says hello again and I say a hello back to him.

So then the guy says to me that his dog bit that license woman's ass. The man smiles with top-level implant teeth, smiles 'n says that dog's bite only cost him a $250 fine. Then this guy looks at me, checks me out.

Let me tell you something. I may be fifty-something-years-old, but I have a good, firm ass. My butt does not look its age.

And this guy looks at me, like he's considering whether or not my ass is something he's willing to pay a $250 fine for if his dog loses common sense 'n takes a bite of my rear end.

The guy is sort of my type… strong and Burt Lancaster-lookin', but maybe he gets off on watching his dog bite women's asses.

So, with him and his dog checking out my ass, the answer I give the guy and his dog is a growly, "Fuck-off."

That always translates to, "No… thank you."

When I get back to my trailer here in Shoshone, back to my tittie-pink kitchen, when I finally sit down to think about it all, my mind drifted back some years to when I was near-married… and then my mind drifted back to high school… and then I fell asleep.

What do you suppose my most memorable dream was, the one that woke me up?

I dreamed that the Pahrump man's dog was a talking dog. And this biting, talking dog said, "Come back, Ursula, come back. " Like the kid in that old Western movie – *Shane*. "Come back, Ursula, and adopt me. I'll be your pal forever."

(*She looks around her trailer kitchen.*)

Not a bad life here. Take-out meals from the café, money for cigarettes, Wednesday drive to Pahrump…. But maybe not such a good life… if this is all there is at the end of the trail.

(*Pause.*) I'll take my chances. Cause, who knows?

(*Pause… and she pulls off her turban and puts on a frowzy blonde wig, looks in the mirror… looks into the audience… sees someone to her liking… points to him and blows a kiss.*).

Maybe <u>you're</u> my dream lover.

THE END

Red Shuttleworth received a 2017 Tanne Foundation Award for Playwriting and Poetry, enabling him to write *Americana West: A Century of Short Plays and Monologues.*

His poetry collection, *Woe to the Land Shadowing,* won a 2016 Western Heritage Wrangler Award. He is a three-time winner of the Western Writers of America Spur Award for Poetry. *True West* magazine named him "Best Living Western Poet" in 2007.

74284635R00035

Made in the USA
Columbia, SC
11 September 2019